COSMIC
SYMPHONY

A Skeptic, a Scientist, and a Philosopher discuss
the mysterious Cosmic Temple and its equally
mysterious occupant—reasoning and behaving Man.

By

Henry R. Vanderbyll

PHILOSOPHICAL LIBRARY
NEW YORK

COSMIC SYMPHONY

PERSONS OF THE DISCUSSION

A Skeptic   A Scientist   A Philosopher

SCENE: *The philosopher's library,* where the three men meet regularly for the purpose of engaging in a friendly discussion of some subject selected at the preceding meeting. The skeptic and the scientist, reclining comfortably in easy chairs, look at the philosopher who, standing near one end of the library table, turns the pages of a manuscript.

SUBJECT OF THE DISCUSSION: *The Biblical stories of Creation and The Fall of Man.* At the last meeting, the philosopher reluctantly agreed to take the leading part in the present discussion. He has since composed an abridged version of the stories in question, and he is about to read it to his attentive audience.

PHILOSOPHER *(reading from manuscript)*
When Earth was void
and nothing filled the deep,
the Ruler of Immensity gave thought to plans
that should embrace a boundless sweep of universe,
wherein a being made in His own image
should arise from sleep
and marvel much
and tremble at His might
which turned eternal darkness into light!

And at the proper time
His power hurled into the night
the sun and glowing Mars
and shaped a beast- and flower-crowded world
beneath ten thousand times a thousand stars!
And when at last existence lay unfurled
within infinity,
its glory shone as yet for no one
but the Lord alone.

7

And God descended to the Earth
to do his crowning miracle:
from mundane clay He moulded Adam's body,
and He blew the breath of life into him!
There he lay—a living soul
created in the true likeness of the Lord,
yet imprisoned in a mortal body
capable of sin.

And next He caused a heavy sleep
to still our ancestor,
and from beneath his flesh removed a rib.
This instantly became a helpmate, Eve,
predestined to enmesh them
in dark threads of evil and of shame.
And Adam, waking from deep sleep, beheld
the female counterpart of his own self!

In Paradise, the land of bliss,
the Lord housed Adam and Eve
and said to them:
"Eat of the fruit these fertile vales afford,
"but do not touch the single kind
"whose stem holds the enticing apple!"

And the Lord would punish the transgressor
who should eat
the merest fragment of its fragrant meat!

And God walked in the cool and balmy air
of the evening,
while on his belly crept the treacherous serpent
seeking out the fair but timid Eve.
His wily speech soon swept away her caution:
as he sought his lair,
already Eve and Adam blindly ate of
the forbidden fruit.
The hour was late!

For suddenly her nakedness appeared to Eve
a shameful thing,
and Adam's bold surveying glance disturbed her much
and seared her conscience with a burning guilt.
Then rolled God's voice down from the clouds!
And Adam feared its rising wrath
as Earth began to shake
and a great wind caused trees to bend and break:

"By my almighty power

"I made the sun to warm you
"and the moon to light your way.
"The Milky River I compelled to run
"through boundless fields of stars
"that could not stay the measure of my strength.
"I am the One
"who blew into your nostrils living breath,
"that you might be
"beyond the pale of death!

"Come forth, you faithless beings!
"Do not hide in shadows,
"for my eyes are everywhere and see all things!
"Hear! Having disobeyed My one commandment,
"you shall know despair!
"having transgressed against Me
"who abide forever in the heavens and on Earth,
"you shall by suffering redeem your worth!"

And God decreed
that Adam should obtain his bread
by sweat and toil;
that Eve should bear
his every male and female child in pain;

that their descendants should always share
responsibility for Adam's sin
and they should pray for peace and blessedness
while harvesting the fruits of wickedness!

And then He drove the pair from Paradise,
past watchful angels bearing flaming swords.
They walked into the barren world
that lies beyond all bliss.
Compassion was the Lord's
when presently they raised their downcast eyes
and, turning, longingly beheld once more
the Blessed Land.
The past had closed the door!

As God had willed it in His righteous wrath,
so fared the human race that sprang
from Adam and Eve.
Born to walk the luring path leading to sin,
man floundered in the quicksand of evil.
The aftermath of Eden's tragedy
lay like a curse upon the Earth
and all the universe!

11

From time to time a prophet would arise,
inspired by God and moved by destiny,
to counsel human beings
grown too wise in ignorance.
"Turn from iniquity," he urged,
"and seek that holy Paradise
"traded by Adam for the realm of lust!"
But men were deaf
and did the things they must.

They walked in vanity
and swelled with greed
and thought themselves the measure of all things.
But some there were who,
chastened by their need,
turned toward God,
Whose voice with mercy rings for the repenter.
"Mankind shall be freed," thus spoke the Lord,
"by my beloved Son,
"Whose holiness shall stay the Evil One!"

And rapidly His words of comfort spread
from mouth to mouth
and up and down the land.

12

And men and women
by misfortune led to deep despair,
the lame with palsied hand,
the weary and oppressed shedding their tears in vain—
all waited for the day to come
when the Savior should reign in Christendom!

*(Short interval of silence during which the philosopher
places the manuscript on the table and seats himself)*

SKEPTIC　　All myths, perhaps we may agree,
betray the adolescence of the early mind.
Nevertheless, I marvel at the way
it deftly manages to weave and bind its fancies
into patterns.
These convey a simple beauty time cannot destroy
and I, for one, am able to enjoy.
But I protest against the reverence displayed
by men of sound intelligence
for fairy tales and lyric nonsense
spilled at ancient sites that now are rubble-filled!

PHILOSOPHER　Three questions write themselves
upon the sky and all the things on Earth.

13

The first is *Whence?*
the second, *Whither?*
and the third is *Why?*
Nor tell me, it is mental impotence
which fails to answer them!
I shall deny that reason at its best
can sweep away these unformed riddles
that are here to stay!

SKEPTIC   And that makes four!
My own capacity for comprehension being average,
I see no riddles but the one
of sapient man's indulging in a beverage
of fables brewn in grey antiquity.
Its potency is groundless hope and fear
dulling the mind and slowing its career!

PHILOSOPHER   The pace of men and things is never such
as to be judged too little or too much!

SKEPTIC   Returning to your *Whence?*
which, you declare, cannot be answered—
this is my reply:
the scientist, with patience and with care

and with the reasoning we know him by,
reveals that things of which we are aware
at once rise from their shaping yesterdays and
institute tomorrow's novel ways.

SCIENTIST   When man lacked knowledge,
he saw mystery in rain and thunder
and the burst of spring.
For him, the world had neither history nor destiny
and therefore seemed to cling, devoid of meaning,
to an empty sky.
To silence apprehension,
he explained in terms of fancy,
odd and beauty-stained.

But neither object nor phenomenon today withstands
the piercing scrutiny of scientists,
who read the Past upon the Present's face
with reasoned certainty.
The chaos ancient man beheld is gone;
and all the gods and demons that he knew are
laws of Nature demonstrated true!

SCEPTIC   Nevertheless, how many thousands

15

spurn your tested findings and established facts
and from your method of deduction turn
to premise some odd notion which attracts
the struggle-weary who for Heaven yearn!

PHILOSOPHER *(to Skeptic)* Consider that the mass of mankind
bend but little toward learning,
yet desire as fervently as you and I
to lend significance to the Lactean fire,
to sunset-glows,
to landscapes that subtend the rainbow's arc—
in short, to all the sweep of
moving shapes and shadows in the deep!

And if they have one Answer for it all—
what of it, friend?
How far has knowledge gone toward the Source
whence silent æons fall forever
on a boundless cosmos spun from bundled energy?
A circling wall of mystery we face
and ever meet ourselves
completing cycles of defeat!

SCIENTIST I am aware that critics would berate

16

the scientist for failing to provide
the master-key to all that is.
Of late, well-meaning thinkers
have sincerely tried to bridge the several gaps
that separate Belief and Theory.
They fail to see
that each arises from necessity!

SEPTIC   Who can deny that science has erased
the countless question marks
that once defied intelligence
and that the ancients traced on all the things they saw!
With her as guide, man learned to contemplate
a cosmos based on lasting laws.
These rule the universe, which does not bless—
but neither does it curse!

SCIENTIST   The edifice of thought that science builds
is roofless—yes—and will be evermore!
Its building bricks are objects and events
linked causally to "after" and "before";
and hence it rises toward firmaments
it fails to reach
and rests on bedrock-stuff intangible,

yet permanent enough!

Does science formulate *the* answer?
No!
She works within the Cosmic Temple,
made so well and fearfully,
and learns to know the mortar binding
building units, laid haphazardly, it seems.
The units grow into stout pillars flanking
sun-lit halls roofed by the void
on which the starlight falls.

The attic, with its stellar chandeliers,
affords no access to the phantom sky
perceived by sense;
the basement, with the gears that turn the world
and that keep moving by atomic power
stored a billion years,
has no egress.
Yet some would have her see the Temple as a whole.
It cannot be!

PHILOSOPHER When shall we learn
that men have not the same subjectiveness!

Some fearlessly explore the darkness
whence this deep existence came
and strike faint sparks of knowledge at her door.
But most of us are timid ones
who frame the unexplored in a consoling light—
its fuel hope engendered by the night!

SKEPTIC   What are we
that we should distrust the Source of being
and Its all-creative force!

SCIENTIST   I think that we reluctantly divorce
our thoughts from our emotions.
Well I know that stirrings of the heart compose
a force compelling all our reasoning to flow
in pre-established channels.
But, of course, we fail to see
that our own persons hire the mind
to find the truth we most desire!

SKEPTIC   And hence the normal processes of thought
lie dormant in the minds of most of us!
We reason little, lest the answer sought by us
should prove to be foundationless.

19

These facts explain why ancient times have brought,
for us to cherish,
air-drawn fantasies and tales
immortalized in Genesis!

PHILOSOPHER When young,
I too would loudly criticize the Word in Genesis
and sneer at those
who swallowed whole the myth of Paradise.
In fierce contempt I held such men as chose
to earn their bread by spreading hallowed lies!
And then I saw myself the foolish one:
they had an Answer, whereas I had none!

SKEPTIC The Age of Reason
grown articulate in criticism and in common sense;
triumphant science standing at the gate
leading to limited omnipotence—
what have they taught the blindly obstinate?

Their ancient demons whisper in the trees,
their magic spouts a rivulet from rock,
their miracles transform the angry seas
into dry land,

20

their musty notions mock man's knowledge
wrested from the centuries!

PHILOSOPHER A store of knowledge
weighs but little more than none at all,
since it reveals the deep and lasting mystery
which is the core of Being.
Few there are who wake from sleep,
and fewer still who thereupon
explore the unexplorable:
our Genesis as yet remains
the best of theories!

SKEPTIC From mathematics I have learned
to reason step by step from premises
that are self-evident.
Hence I have turned from theories
about the genesis of all that is.
Today I am concerned merely
with things and beings and events,
and antecedents with their consequents.

From science I have learned
that all the known was built

21   ·

by the observing, curious mind.
I reach for solid facts
and leave alone their wishful counterfeits.
And now I find,
the scanty known I started with has grown
into a universe of stars and men
to which no *whence* applies, no *where,* no *when!*

In mental comfort I observe the whole
that once unnerved me
as it bored its mystery into my timid soul;
for pioneering Reason has explored
the contents of the star-lit rimless bowl
in which I have my being
and reflect upon the marvel of the human intellect.

The time-worn cup of life disintegrates unheeded:
it is filled unto the brim with Nature's wonders,
which she dedicates to the inquiring mind;
and all the arbitrary doings of the Fates
but weakly shake my psyche reaching for
the space-locked secret of the meteor!

PHILOSOPHER How well I know the road you travel, friend—

22

its solid surface
hardened by the touch of common sense,
its every fork and bend,
its milestones marked for those
who very much desire to fathom and to comprehend:
the road of science
built of lasting stuff
making it critic-proof and safe enough!

I too am fond of scientific lore,
and sweep riddles from the multiverse
man sees with flesh-bound eyes.
I daily do the chore of dusting fancies
from the Pleiades and Perseus.
At times I seek the shore
of Scorpio's remotest galaxy,
and I ride lightbeams in immensity.

Of late, however, as the years decline,
I sweep less hopefully,
for bounds recede as feebly I continue to define!
So little time is left,
so much I need,
to finish that unending chore of mine!

23

I think the thousand riddles swept away
make One Great Riddle
which is here to stay!

I think the many simple mysteries of ancient times
have blended into One
encompassing the Earth and brooding skies.
Nor tell me, friend,
that factual knowledge won for me
what lack of scholarship denies!
For all my learning
helps me not a bit to measure space
and weigh the infinite!

SCIENTIST   A faulty concept—that of endlessness,
perhaps corrected by the theory of curving space
or by the clever guess that Time unwinds
the super-galaxy which is the world!
Their truth, I must confess,
I cannot prove without the piercing eye of Palomar
seeking a bounded sky.

PHILOSOPHER Be men dull-witted or intelligent,
illiterate or too profoundly learned,

24

alike they sense themselves incompetent
to measure that which cannot be discerned;
to dwell upon a phantom firmament;
to find a *whither* when there is no *whence*;
to link the Little with the One Immense!

We are but children
viewing Palomar's gigantic eye
in wish-engendered hope
that it may pierce the *Horse's Head* *
barring our vision
from the bounds for which we grope.
As if the cosmic temple of the stars
were roofed and walled
and built on shifting clay,
and boundlessness were but a word we say!

(*Short interval of silence, during which the Skeptic
apparently reflects upon the Philosopher's views of
the nature of the universe*)

SKEPTIC   The calculus is better to my taste

---

* Dark nebula, shaped like the head of a horse, in Orion's great nebula.

and much more restful
than the measureless you find or run from
in the star-lit waste of cosmic space!
The skills and thoroughness of mathematics
cannot be replaced
as stepping stones to solid certainties
inhering in the given quantities!

PHILOSOPHER There is an indefinable sublime
that serves as basis for your postulates
and quickens theories of space and time!
Your calculus, with its related rates
and ordinates that steeply fall or climb
in futile search of twin infinities,
faintly whispers of the eternities!

I put away the slide rule, pen and ink,
and cease to measure, weigh, and calculate
(and so do honest men who live to think)
when my dim path of thought
at last has led me to the end!
I stand upon the brink of the unbounded,
where Existence *is*—
without a future or a genesis!

26

(Short interval of silence)

SKEPTIC   Were each of us half-willing
to amend his private views
and practice tolerance,
our argument might reach a happy end.
Alas, I cannot suffer ignorance
which men applaud and piously defend!

SCIENTIST   I likewise am unable to approve
such crooked reasoning as circumvents
the rigid test.
Necessity and love for knowledge
sometimes prompt me to invent hypotheses
by which I swiftly move to explanations.
These I will retract,
should they conflict with but a single fact!

PHILOSOPHER Men are so constituted as to see or not to see,
according to their lights.
A few behold a cosmic mystery,
while many contemplate from humbler heights
a simple world.
But each describes for me the scene he views

27

and tells me how he fills the void
whence spring the stars and daffodils.

Shall I, who contemplate a different scene
and recognize the void as part of it,
inform my neighbor that his lights
have been too dim for reading clearly?
Never yet has argument destroyed the link
between the Seer and the Seen!
For it was wrought at birth
from the endowments Nature brought.

The very little men perceive
they dress in Reason's garment,
trimmed with hope and lined with faith
to compensate for scantiness.
No fruit, except perhaps the bitter kind,
results from scorn the critic may express:
he might with profit quit his puny heights
to view the world according to their lights!

SKEPTIC   A queer philosopher is he, I think,
who idly views the spectacle
of man's seeking the light of knowledge

in the realm of dark credulity!
No doubt, he can instruct him in such basic facts
as link the mind with understanding.
Of what use learning
that fails to sharpen the obtuse!

IILOSOPHER Are minds then vessels filled by me at will
with my own view of things?
The pupil makes the teacher,
the second not the first!
Still, some there are who from my musings take
such thoughts as please them
and exactly fill a need.
In teaching, too, this rule is first:
men drink or don't, according as they thirst!

EPTIC And so we must continue to accept the void
as the dark cradle from which leaped
the fire of stars that sparked the intellect!

IILOSOPHER Instruction of mankind
should never lead to guessing
as to how the world was made!
An Answer?

29

Yes, perhaps.
It would indeed be stuff for men
who at ripe age have paid
with toil and tears for life on Earth!
They need a buoyant hope!
The truth?
Well, let it be of less importance than
the truths men see!

The sound philosopher perceives the fact
that thinking is a private enterprise.
What if its fruit be mostly sear or cracked
in the opinion of the would-be wise?
It pleases owners
who at once react with bitter fury
to destructive blasts from
thoughtless critics and iconoclasts!

No wise man ever tries to bring round
a thoroughly convinced humanity.
Their thoughts, be they inaccurate or sound,
describe such worlds
as they have come to see by nature.
Some think existence matter-bound

and, others, spirit-moved:
the wise man knows that
many differing petals make the rose!

(*Interval of silence. The skeptic, regarding the philosopher, apparently has been impressed by the arguments of his opponent*)

SKEPTIC   (*to Philosopher*)
You have half-converted me to your views,
and only half!
We do not merely think:
we act in ways
that utterly confuse my simple mind.
Is there perhaps a link binding our thought
to conduct?
I refuse, of course, such stories as *The Fall!*
They rank with fables
and forever keep mankind proving a truth
which reason cannot find!

PHILOSOPHER (*to Skeptic*)
My friend, has this perhaps occurred to you:
the spirit of your fable

31

lends its fire to meaning,
which consumes the letter.
True, the snake is inarticulate,
but Desire is not,
as loudly it demands its due!
Immune these ancient stories to
the sting of logic!
Ever new the truth they bring!

The lasting ones successfully portray
our blindly groping selves
forever bent upon
attaining goals without delay.
They subtly show that moments spent in anguish
are self-made;
and we regret that we are we
and that we are not yet!

SKEPTIC   All of us behave, I am well aware,
as if directed by the hand of Sin.
No honest man, I am convinced,
would dare proclaim his own perfection!
Yet, within the bounds of reason,
I would answer this:

32

what *is* this sin and what its genesis?

SCIENTIST   Nowhere in all the universe
one finds an evil force determining our fate!
Why then in man
whose basic nature binds him to the cosmos?
Yet, his moral state is found to be established
by the kinds of complex compounds, glands, and nerves
that move his guiltless person toward hate or love.

Reason seeks neither innocence nor guilt
in man's behavior and activities!
It seeks the makers of the crazy-quilt
which is his life.
These are such qualities of blood and brain
as mark his moral build
and launch him on a bright or dark career
achieved by confidence or wrecked by fear!

SKEPTIC   (*to Scientist*)
You fail to mention the environment,
another maker of your crazy-quilt!

SCIENTIST   Yes, the environment!

33

Of late, it has
banished the devil and usurped his throne
and now is driving to their moral fate
all evildoers!
Far worse than none
half-theories causing to disintegrate
the social whole to which they are applied!
Of course, what must be proved
must first be tried!

SKEPTIC   (*to Scientist*)
The other half concerns the inner man?

SCIENTIST   Precisely!
Unlike things withstand the test of fire
in differing ways:
some are destroyed,
some burned or lightly scorched,
whereas the rest will gain in strength.
A few brave men,
employed in gainful labor at their own request,
are lame or sightless.
The environment thus far
has failed to halt the competent!

34

PHILOSOPHER There is much truth in everything you say—
much obvious truth, I think.
For qualities of mind and soul
are as the surface spray
concealing shoals and depths in entities
called individuals.
What *is* the wind? Our answer is: it blows!

(*Short interval of silence during which the philosopher
weighs his next words*)

PHILOSOPHER When life first quivered in the cosmic deep,
the creature did not know the glories strewn
from Earth to the Lactea.
It was asleep and yet awake;
for hearing the shrill tune of its own need,
it foraged for its keep
in a dark world hewn from chaos.
Aware of self,
how could it know the comet's flare?

When ages later
the First Man emerged from Nature's womb,
one more somnambulist moved in the dark.

35

The cosmos lay submerged in dawning reason.
All his poor thought converged upon the problem
of quenching his thirst and stilling his hunger
The self was first!

As yet, men walk as if in sleep
and see in many instances
but little more than private interest.
For it can be that they know little more
than the locked door delaying pleasure,
the harsh melody of hope deferred—
frustration's pang that dims
the Cosmic Temple humming lasting hymns!

SKEPTIC   (*agitatedly*)
Very clever!
Your thought for me implies
that we as yet would look at skies and stars
without perceiving them!
We exercise our minds but little:
waging private wars and brewing little schemes
promoted by Desire,
we rob our minds of liberty!
Yet, some I know

who, looking, clearly see.

And that sublime inventor called the mind—
what does it scheme for us?
The shortest way,
be it muddy or clean,
by which the blind may reach their goal!
Our reason, checked by clay,
is servant to our self!
How shall it find solutions of the problems
that beset our groping soul
enmeshed in its own net?

Can we perceive the truth whose ears are made
for sounds of self-concern;
whose eyes seek out
such luring pleasures as must quickly fade;
whose reasoned projects
merely bring about self-pampering?
Our grain is of a grade preventing thought
from probing that which lies beyond
the bounds of our fool's paradise!

SCIENTIST   Often it has been said

37

that stars are cold
and cosmic space blankets the soul with frost.
These things must be,
since scientists behold a world
in which their logic soon gets lost
when swayed by the emotions.
Truth unfolds itself for him
whose person stands aloof,
as reason fumbles, posits, and seeks proof!

PHILOSOPHER (*to Scientist*)
I have suggested, merely,
that life by slow and gradual stages
rose from cosmic sleep;
that, as it woke, the world it got to know
. grew at the same rate.
The vast star-lit deep,
with unseen energies that form and flow,
is home for some;
but most of us abide in lesser worlds—
self-made and self-decried!

SKEPTIC A little higher than the beast we are,
because so fashioned as to see

the cloud obscure the moon
and the evening star drop into her silver bowl.
But very loud the carnal self
re-enacting a scene
from the stark drama of the Pliocene!

SCIENTIST   In all of us
slumbers the memory of bygone ages,
when the saber-tooth
the crushing paw,
the lethal armory of moving flesh,
established the grim truth which then prevailed.
No such unsavory tools are ours;
but reason may crush fellow beings
in a cunning way!

The origin of sin?
It coincides with that of life!
Your so-called evil sleeps in its strange shapes
and finally resides in Nature's prodigy,
who laughs and weeps
and covets treasure that the rainbow hides.
In him it thrives,
until at last his mind perceives

39

that too much self destroys mankind!

SKEPTIC   A moral being!
            Thus one ill-defines the creature
            who continually creates disturbances on Earth!
            His greed outlines the face of history,
            his lust inflates her aging body,
            and his evil shines
            like burning fever in her tired eyes—
            all this, because he does not think, nor tries!

PHILOSOPHER (*to Skeptic*)
            Be not unjust!
            Men think little or much because they must.
            Thoughts are like garments
            that fit perfectly the inner man   .
            and thus reveal the world
            each knows subjectively.
            Our scientist,
            by Nature made to feel a vast existence
            few of us may see and know,
            gives speech to his awareness.
            And so, the story of the world is told!

40

SKEPTIC   Awareness?
               Well I know the kind of man
               who thinks only when urgency compels,
               or hope entices,
               or temptations fan the embers of desire!
               Reason he sells for fleeting comfort
               in the caravan of circumstances.
               Whence *his* awareness
               thus self-imprisoned in the measureless?

PHILOSOPHER   Man's feeble mind was made
               for measuring impermanence.
               He counts the years that fade forever,
               weighs the dust clouds gathering in empty space,
               and builds a balustrade of facts and figures
               whence to seize the wing of wingless time.
               And yet he would discern such matters
               as are none of his concern!

SCIENTIST   (*to Skeptic*)
               Scientists teach those who may wish to read
               that all distinctions arise from sameness.
               The multiform
               lies dormant in the seed of homogeneity,

41

and the "less" and "more,"
the "worse" and "better"—
these proceed from uniformity.
Diversity, rather than quantity,
is Nature's aim!

PHILOSOPHER Some may say that all things differentiate
and others that the Cosmic Architect
creates unceasingly.
At any rate, variety of heart and intellect
most certainly exists.
Investigate this mystery:
eventually you may find
the omnipresence of a Perfect Mind!

I say again:
all men somnambulate beneath the stars;
but some, whose sleep is light,
experience waking moments
when they rate Not-Self higher than the Self.
And the night in which they tend to walk
will dissipate,
since their awareness of the universe
muzzles the flesh and checks the age-old curse!

42

What man who has explored but hurriedly
Creation's field
will trample underfoot the forest lily
(as does the jungle beast unknowingly)
avidly compute his shady gains,
ignore his neighbor's cry of fear and agony,
and desecrate the Cosmic Temple
with the sound of hate!

(*Interval of silence*)

SKEPTIC   (*to Philosopher*)
Quite well presented is your theory
and clothed in beauty, too!
I must concede
that you have demonstrated life to be
a drama of strange splendor
which, indeed, I cannot dim
by sparring cleverly in debate.
Nevertheless, I am I
and am constrained to think accordingly!

SCIENTIST   (*to Philosopher*)
Your reasoning and eloquence

43

I, too, find to my taste.
But Nature has assigned to me
a boundless field, surveyed by few,
in which I labor.
The mental tools designed by her—
these I must employ,
even as you must use your own.
To each his field, his labor,
and the harvest that they yield!

SKEPTIC   What natural field may possibly be mine!
I deeply relish halting in their flight
such wishful fancies as would undermine
the strength of reasoning,
and with delight I fence and argue with
the Philistine promoter of some truth
rooting in air.
The harvest?
Barren soil—what can it bear?

SCIENTIST   (*to Skeptic*)
A follower of science, you should learn
that men's beliefs must be their own concern!

PHILOSOPHER   (*to Skeptic*)

44

Skeptics are half-philosophers
impressed profoundly by
their proper reasoning and view of things!
The famous ones have dressed their ire in beauty
or blunted the sting of criticism
by their sharp wit.
At best,
they have quite thoroughly convinced themselves
in empty volumes weighing down on shelves!

KEPTIC   (*to Philosopher, with mild sarcasm*)
Before our wandering discussion ends,
kindly enlighten me!
What, then, may be *your* view of things?
At times I think it bends toward the scientist,
at times I see it blend with mine,
and then again it lends support
to all the wish-philosophies
that breed beliefs as well as heresies!

PHILOSOPHER (*earnestly*)
Of course, I am a human being first,
knowing great joy as well as suffering.
I too am light with hope

45

and sometimes thirst for things
that rouse Desire when slumbering.
Also frustration now and then would burst
the dam impounding my emotions.
Can I then be blind
to what concerns my fellow men?

I stand behind them
as they contemplate the world
and in their ways interpret it.
I feel with them the shifting hand of Fate,
the buoyant touch of hope,
the closing net of circumstance,
and joys that alternate with pain.
I too entrust my soul to deity,
Who made and rules the whole!

Also behind the scientist I stand
and with him ponder the power-laden world
of protons and electrons,
and the Hand that moves Arcturus
and that once unfurled the spiral nebula
and drew the band of the vast Milky Way
across the sky:

both common man and scientist am I!

Last of all, I am the philosopher,
without a view that I may call my own—
except when I am Self, and little more.
Then I dispraise the Sower and the Sown,
while finding many things
that should be more in keeping with my taste.
Yes, I possess a view of things—
but narrow, more or less.

Quite frequently, the carping Self retires,
permitting thought to be unchained and free:
I have no view,
but clearly see the frosts and fires
that chill and burn humanity.
I see the steady light the scientist requires
for reading secrets of the universe.
I have no view,
but find I am not worse than others
who possess and advertise the truth they see
while frowning on the one
who in his blindness visions otherwise!
I will not argue with my fellow men

who seek security in faith
or devise odd pillars for support.
I shall respect their truth,
though it defy the intellect!

SKEPTIC   I *am* confused!
Does it not matter, then,
whether or not our deity be real?
I find it odd that you leave fellow men
to revere their images!
Why not appeal to common sense
so well employed by them
for private purposes!

PHILOSOPHER Have you not read:
No man has ever seen the face of God?
Philosophers who are and who have been
have vainly tried to find the Real
by rending veils of mist behind the cosmic scene.
A poet warned: ". . . presume not God to scan: °
"the proper study for mankind is man!"

Sufficient for defining beings is
the certain knowledge

that the Architect has blueprinted
and still is shaping this existence!
The measuring intellect,
when qualifying Him Who ever IS,
employs such terms as name the things
we see on our own level of mortality!

Do not define the Ultimate!
Instead, read in your brother's eyes
the drowsiness that blurs Creation,
with its marvels spread
between his nodding Self and endlessness!
As yet a child,
he is by nature led to spin his fancies,
to indulge desire,
and innocently to play with fire!

When viewing the human world about you
and feeling its heat of friction,
hear the voice of Wisdom plead:
". . . they know not what they do!"
Men see but see not,
choose but have no choice,
sin but are not guilty.

All but a few
have not yet waked to see reality
in all-encompassing infinity!

I say to you:
you may condemn the act
but not the actor;
you may reject thought
but not the thinker!
You should perceive the fact that every man
unknowingly is brought by his own nature
faithfully to act the role assigned to him.
By Whom or What?
Let your own mind and conscience answer that!

SKEPTIC   (*Glances at his watch. Rises. Approaches Philosopher*)
A fruitful evening,
though I must confess my inability
to name its fruit.
What knowledge may you possibly possess
our scientist and I can not refute!
What *do* you know besides the wilderness
whose flickering stars and flaring comets
light Life's flimsy bridge

50

suspending in the night!

Somehow, I am disturbed by gnawing doubt—
I who until this evening tread on ground
well-tamped with facts
and managed to turn out,
by force of logic,
thoughts that are unsound.
But now the ground is softening all about
and facts are muddied by uncertainty!
What power, good or evil, may be yours?

PHILOSOPHER (*to Skeptic*)
The placid waters of philosophy
seek their humble source in skepticism.
Cling to the facts, my friend,
but think before you build with them!
The scientist, of course,
does it revealingly and skillfully—
but is he critical of the Plan
he gradually unfolds for curious man?

In one respect,
you obviously depart from scientific ways.

51

If facts are real
and you would not exchange them
for the art of hiding them,
why spurn them when you deal with fellow men?
Such is the human heart
and such the mind:
either accept the Plan
or alter it by carping—
if you can!

Build *on* your facts—on stark reality!
True thinkers firmly stand in
what appears to be Life's gutter;
watch reflectively Folly's bubbles,
the scum of Sin,
and tears that carry them away;
then seek the sky
whose bright light, falling on the scene,
reveals deep truths
which surface evidence conceals.

(*Interval of silence*)

SKEPTIC   (*to Philosopher*)

52

Strange man!
I believe that you have caused to crack
the strong foundations of my house of thought,
which needs remodeling.
I may return a wiser man
who views mankind
without those mental glasses colored almost black
by his biased Self!
Long have I known that many wear them and
hence project their deep desires and grievances
upon the screen of this existence!
Biting ridicule I have employed
to make them choose between
such reasoning as is emotion's tool
and such as is the mind's!
Had I not been blinded by Self,
I should have understood that Nature's works
are neither bad nor good!

SCIENTIST   *(rising)*
I must be off!
A pleasant evening, for which I thank you both!
To my surprise I find
that scientific reasoning

53

helps men of differing views to compromise!
Philosopher or skeptic—
each would ring his field of thought
with penetrating light
such as science generates.
Well, good night!

(*Philosopher rises. The three men move toward the open door and into the hall. The front door audibly closes. Philosopher re-enters.*)

PHILOSOPHER A fruitful evening!

The End

CPSIA information can be obtained
at www.ICGtesting.com
Printed in the USA
BVHW071447140819
555886BV00010B/319/P